PLATFORM GAMES

By
Kirsty Holmes

 **CRABTREE**
PUBLISHING COMPANY
WWW.CRABTREEBOOKS.COM

CRABTREE
PUBLISHING COMPANY
WWW.CRABTREEBOOKS.COM

Published
in Canada
Crabtree Publishing
616 Welland Avenue
St. Catharines, ON
L2M 5V6

Published in
the United States
Crabtree Publishing
PMB 59051
350 Fifth Ave, 59th Floor
New York, NY 10118

Published in 2019 by Crabtree Publishing Company

Author: Kirsty Holmes

Editors: Holly Duhig, Petrice Custance

Design: Gareth Liddington

Proofreader: Melissa Boyce

**Production coordinator and
 prepress technician:** Margaret Amy Salter

Print coordinator: Katherine Berti

Photo credits:
All images are courtesy of Shutterstock.com.

Cover – , 2 – Swill Klitch, 4 – Swill Klitch, 5 – Giuseppe_R, Saikorn, Niphon Subsri, 10 – Blan-k, A-spring, Prostock-studio, adamziaja.com, 11 – GooGag, IconBunny, 18 – VitalityVill, 22 – pluie_r, 23 – Evan-Amos, Boffy b. Images are courtesy of Shutterstock.com. With thanks to Getty Images, Thinkstock Photo and iStockphoto.

Sonic the Hedgehog: All images courtesy of Sega Games Co (SEGA), all rights reserved. With grateful thanks.

Bit.Trip Runner series: All images courtesy of Choice Provisions., all rights reserved. With grateful thanks.

LittleBigPlanet: All images courtesy of Sony Interactive Entertainment, all rights reserved. With grateful thanks.

Starbound: All images courtesy of Chucklefish (c)., all rights reserved. With grateful thanks to Rosie Ball.

All facts, statistics, web addresses and URLs in this book were verified as valid and accurate at time of writing. No responsibility for any changes to external websites or references can be accepted by either the author or publisher.

Printed in the U.S.A./012019/CG20181123

Library and Archives Canada Cataloguing in Publication

Holmes, Kirsty, author
        Platform games / Kirsty Holmes.

(Game on!)
Includes index.
Issued in print and electronic formats.
ISBN 978-0-7787-5259-2 (hardcover).--
ISBN 978-0-7787-5272-1 (softcover).--
ISBN 978-1-4271-2188-2 (HTML)

        1. Video games--Juvenile literature. 2. Computer adventure games--Juvenile literature. I. Title.

GV1469.22.H645 2019   j794.8'4582   C2018-906127-8
                                                                                C2018-906128-6

Library of Congress Cataloging-in-Publication Data

Names: Holmes, Kirsty, author.
Title: Platform games / Kirsty Holmes.
Description: New York, New York : Crabtree Publishing Company, 2019. |
    Series: Game on! | Includes index.
Identifiers: LCCN 2018053426 (print) | LCCN 2018055654 (ebook) |
    ISBN 9781427121882 (Electronic) |
    ISBN 9780778752592 (hardcover : alk. paper) |
    ISBN 9780778752721 (pbk. : alk. paper)
Subjects: LCSH: Video games--Juvenile literature. |
    Computer adventure games--Juvenile literature.
Classification: LCC GV1469.3 (ebook) | LCC GV1469.3 .H677 2019 (print) |
    DDC 794.8--dc23
LC record available at https://lccn.loc.gov/2018053426

CONTENTS

WELCOME TO THE ARCADE

Have you got ninja-like **reflexes**, superhuman shooting skills, and really **nimble** thumbs? Then you were made to win at platform games! You've probably already played a bit, and maybe you're pretty good, but this gaming guide will level up your knowledge to take you from a beginner to a know-it-all in no time. So fire up your joystick and get comfy. It's time to get your game on!

Hey, new player! I LOVE gaming. Let's find out all we can about platform games. We can use the Arcade—it's a supercomputer and it's really cool. Are you ready? Let's go!

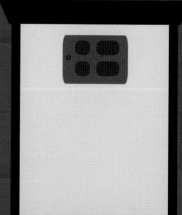

Let's start with the basics. A video game is an **electronic** game that needs a player (that's you!) to use a device to make stuff happen on a screen. Usually that screen is on a television or a personal computer (PC), but you can play games on smartphones, handheld gaming devices, or tablets. To play on your television you will need a **console**. There are many types of video games—from thrilling sports games to **battle royale** games that will see you risking your **virtual** life. There is something for everyone in a video game!

We have a lot of running and jumping ahead of us. Are you ready? Okay, Arcade, let's begin!

<<Player One... Ready...?>>

ARCADE

DATA FILE: PLATFORM GAMES

Okay, Arcade, please load data.

<<LOADING... DATA LEVEL ONE: WHAT IS A PLATFORM GAME?>>

A platform game is a type of action game. The player controls a character who must travel across a series of platforms, avoiding **obstacles** and enemies, either to make it to the next level or achieve an **objective**. The player controls their character to run, jump, climb ladders, swing on ropes, and avoid traps or spikes to complete the level. Often there are collectibles, or items which are valuable or useful, for the player to collect along the way. Collectibles may be worth points or may give special abilities, health points, or extra lives.

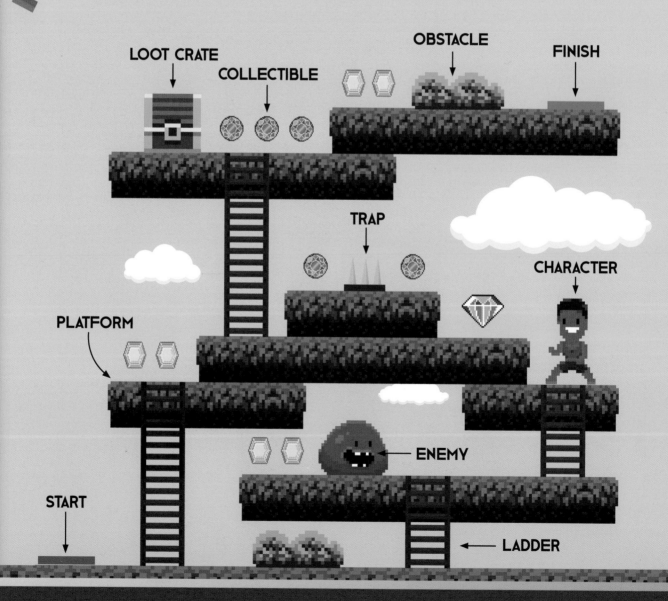

LOOT CRATE

COLLECTIBLE

OBSTACLE

FINISH

TRAP

PLATFORM

CHARACTER

ENEMY

START

LADDER

PUZZLE PLATFORMER

These games use a platform style, but most of the gameplay takes the form of puzzles to solve.

RUN-AND-GUN

Sometimes called platform shooters, these games are all about the guns. Players have to shoot their enemies while running along the platforms.

CINEMATIC PLATFORMER

These games use realistic **graphics** to create beautiful, movie-quality games.

ENDLESS RUNNER

The player never stops running! The levels can go on forever and the player must jump, climb, and swing, but can never stop!

SIDE-SCROLLING

Games where the screen moves across sideways as the player moves through the level.

PLATFORM-ADVENTURE

These games use a platform style, but include elements of adventure games too.

3-D PLATFORMERS

A **3-D** platform game allows the player to see the action as if they are the character in the game.

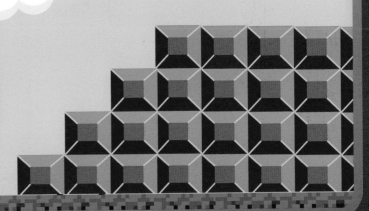

FACT FILE: SUPER MARIO BROS.

If there's one character that stands above the rest in the game world, it's Nintendo's lovable plumber, Mario. His first appearance in a video game was in the famous and classic game Donkey Kong, but he wasn't called Mario. Back then, Mario was called Jumpman. It didn't take long for Nintendo to realize that this new hero was a star in the making, and the little red plumber appeared a couple of years later in his own adventure.

From there, Mario has never looked back. He has starred in countless games, many of which have **defined** platform games. In Super Mario Bros., which launched on the Nintendo Entertainment System in 1985, gaming's leading man became the icon for a **generation** and the star of several side-scrolling platform greats.

In 1996, Mario once again changed the gaming world with Super Mario 64, which was one of the first games to land on the N64 console. In fact, Mario has featured in games for all of Nintendo's consoles, including its latest, the Nintendo Switch. Super Mario Odyssey is the newest adventure in the series, and some people have even gone as far as to call it the best game ever made!

Of course, Mario is the main man, but let's not forget his brother, Luigi, his friends, Princess Peach and Toad, and even his trusty companion, Yoshi. Mario truly has some of the best friends in gaming. He's got one of the most fearsome enemies too. Bowser is always up to some sort of mischief in the Mushroom Kingdom! Mario and his friends have appeared in TV shows and movies, and they're even going to come to life when Nintendo opens its own theme parks. As long as Nintendo keeps making great games, there's no chance of Mario going anywhere. He's the king for a reason.

TECH TALK

If you're going to be good at platform games, you need to know what you're talking about. This data file is crammed with lots of information about this type of game. Let's take a look. Arcade, tell us what we need to know.

<<LOADING... DATA LEVEL THREE: WHAT YOU NEED TO KNOW>>

PLAYER INFO

Play in one-player or two-player modes, either online or on the same console with two controllers. Some games even offer play for a group of players at once! In two-player mode, the screen might split into two, or you might play on the same screen.

ADD-ONS

Add-ons are things you can plug into the console or PC to add functions to the game. Most platform games only need the basic controllers that come with your game. If you are playing online, you will need a headset to talk to other players. If you play on a touchscreen device, then you don't need add-ons.

VISUALS

Most platform games take place on a single path, with lots of levels and platforms the player must cross or use. Some are flat worlds and some are 3-D. Graphics can be simple **pixelated** images or beautiful artworks. Levels can take place on a single, fixed screen or a side-scrolling landscape.

CONTROLS

The most important control in any platformer is the JUMP button. Jumping gets you from level to level. In some games, your only attack is jumping on enemies, so practice this a lot! Next up is FIRE, which is handy for taking out enemies with a fireball or two. More advanced controls include swinging, climbing, or bouncing on trampolines.

LEVELS

Most games will offer a **tutorial** level to help you learn the controls. The first levels will usually be quite easy, but the game will slowly become harder as you progress to higher levels. This is called a learning curve. If games didn't get harder, you'd soon get bored! The hardest levels are called boss levels. Here, you meet a very tough enemy and must defeat them to progress.

FACT FILE: SONIC MANIA

Sega's blue hedgehog is one of the most famous characters in the gaming world. Even if you've never run a loop-de-loop in his shoes, you've probably watched him on television or seen his face in a magazine. Sonic became a household name, thanks to his fast feet and funky attitude, and it certainly helps that he's got one of the catchiest theme tunes around!

Sonic became such a huge star in the gaming world that he started appearing in all sorts of different types of games. So far, he's starred in his own Olympic Games alongside Mario, and in racing games, pinball games, and even 3-D action-adventure games. Sonic is still a popular character and it doesn't look like he's going to slow down anytime soon.

Sonic started life as a platform hero. He runs through levels at super speeds, grabs all the gold rings he can, spins into his enemies, avoids dangerous spikes, and squares off against Doctor Robotnik—also known as Doctor Eggman—in challenging boss battles. Sonic may jump on the heads of his enemies, but in the end, he is saving the local wildlife that has been transformed by the evil Doctor.

When Sonic isn't jumping on platforms and dodging enemies, he is looking for secrets hidden throughout the levels. On top of the many gold rings, there are **power-ups** that give Sonic a shield, make him **invincible**, or make him run even faster!

Sonic started off on his own, but in the second game of the series he was joined by his trusty friend, Miles "Tails" Prower. Tails was the first in a growing cast of characters that would join the lightning-quick hedgehog in adventures, including Amy Rose and Knuckles the Echidna.

TIMELINE OF PLATFORM GAMES

Time for a history lesson. We'll need to access the archives for this one. Arcade, please access and display timeline files.

START

<<LOADING... DATA LEVEL FOUR: PLATFORM GAMES TIMELINE>>

EARLY 1980s

Although other games such as Space Panic and Crazy Climber existed, most people think the first platform game was Nintendo's Donkey Kong, which was released in 1981. In 1983, Mario Bros. was released. Most of these games had a fixed screen and the goal was to climb the platforms to the top.

LATE 1980s

Side-scrolling gameplay started to become popular with the release of Super Mario Bros. This game became the leader of the **genre**, with many similar games coming out soon after. Handheld consoles, such as the Nintendo Game Boy and Sega Game Gear, put platforming in people's pockets.

EARLY 1990s

Better technology in consoles led to more difficult games. Sonic the Hedgehog was released in 1991 by Sega, rocketing platformers into the 1990s with breakneck speed. Games such as Prince of Persia pushed the limits of animation and appealed to older players too.

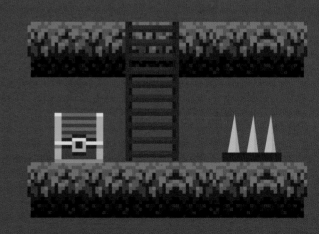

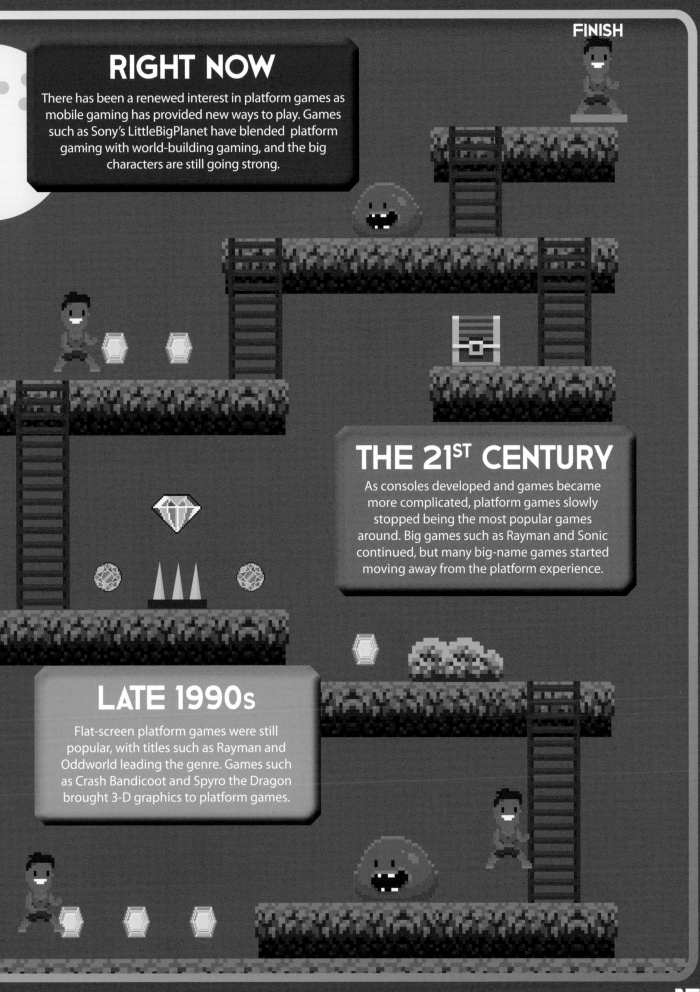

FINISH

RIGHT NOW

There has been a renewed interest in platform games as mobile gaming has provided new ways to play. Games such as Sony's LittleBigPlanet have blended platform gaming with world-building gaming, and the big characters are still going strong.

THE 21ST CENTURY

As consoles developed and games became more complicated, platform games slowly stopped being the most popular games around. Big games such as Rayman and Sonic continued, but many big-name games started moving away from the platform experience.

LATE 1990s

Flat-screen platform games were still popular, with titles such as Rayman and Oddworld leading the genre. Games such as Crash Bandicoot and Spyro the Dragon brought 3-D graphics to platform games.

FACT FILE: RUNNER 3

Not all games are made by studios with dozens (or sometimes hundreds) of employees. There are many smaller studios out there making great games. You've probably played some! These smaller teams of developers are often referred to as indies, or independents, and one of these indie studios is called Choice Provisions.

Choice Provisions made its name by making a number of similar-looking games in what they called the BIT. TRIP series. One of the games in that series was called BIT. TRIP Runner. The game had pixelated graphics and starred a quirky little character by the name of CommanderVideo.

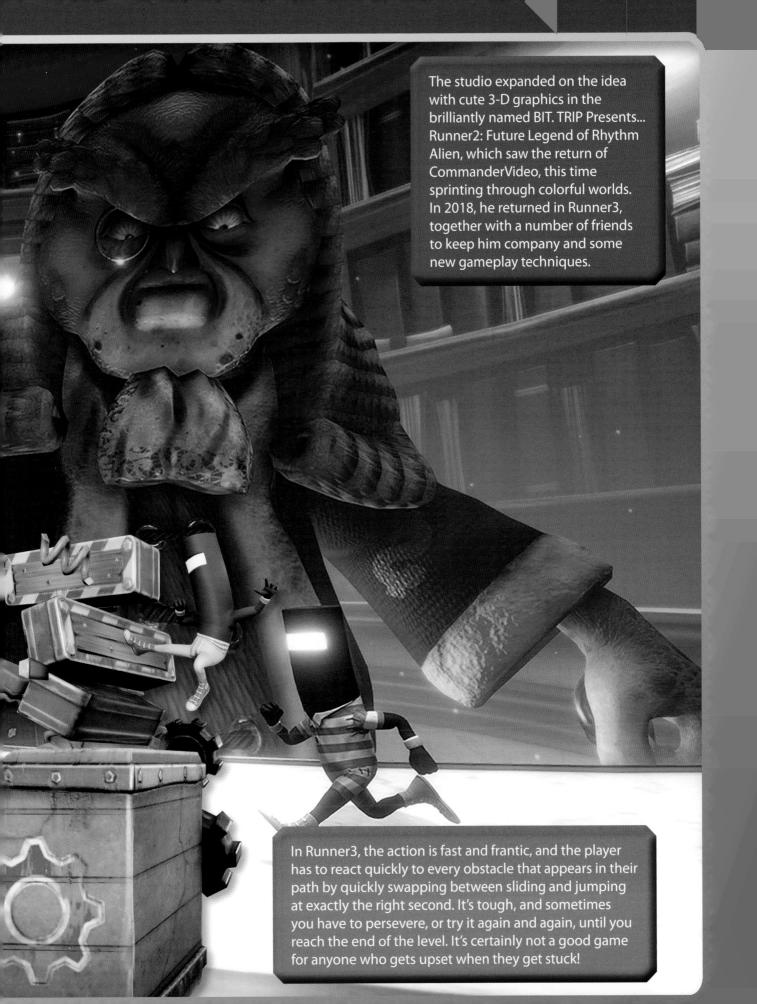

The studio expanded on the idea with cute 3-D graphics in the brilliantly named BIT. TRIP Presents... Runner2: Future Legend of Rhythm Alien, which saw the return of CommanderVideo, this time sprinting through colorful worlds. In 2018, he returned in Runner3, together with a number of friends to keep him company and some new gameplay techniques.

In Runner3, the action is fast and frantic, and the player has to react quickly to every obstacle that appears in their path by quickly swapping between sliding and jumping at exactly the right second. It's tough, and sometimes you have to persevere, or try it again and again, until you reach the end of the level. It's certainly not a good game for anyone who gets upset when they get stuck!

GET YOUR GAME ON

It's time to play. Load up your platform game, stretch out those thumbs, and get comfy. Okay, Arcade, please load the gaming guide.

<<LOADING... DATA LEVEL FIVE: HOW TO PLAY>>

PRESS START TO BEGIN

If you're new to platforming, choose a game and play the tutorial carefully to learn the controls you will need to play. If you have more experience, see if your game has difficulty settings ranging from EASY to IMPOSSIBLE. A game can feel totally different on a harder setting.

OBJECTIVES

The aim of the game is known as your objective. This will be different from game to game, so make sure you know what you're trying to achieve. Maybe you have to complete the level as quickly as possible. Perhaps there's someone in distress to rescue, or you have to find all the collectibles before you can leave. Knowing this will help you plan your **strategy**.

YOU LOST A LIFE

Platform games often require trial-and-error, meaning you will probably die many times in the game before you can complete a level. Make sure you save your game whenever you can. Some games will give you a certain number of lives, or a set amount of times you can receive a fatal injury before it's GAME OVER. Others will have a health bar that will decrease each time you are injured until it's empty, and then it's GAME OVER. Some games have permadeath, which means it's GAME OVER the first time you die. Find out which collectible gives you an extra life, and collect as many of them as you can. Otherwise—you guessed it— it's GAME OVER!

PATTERN POWER

Platform games are all about patterns. Look for the timing of an enemy movement. Often an enemy will move back and forth across a small area in a repeating pattern, so knowing this pattern is key to getting past it. But enemies aren't your only problem when jumping through your level. In a platform game, you are more likely to die from a badly timed jump that lands you in a pit of spikes or a bottomless pit.

<<DID YOU KNOW?>>
PRACTICE, PRACTICE, PRACTICE! THE MORE YOU PLAY AND LEARN THE PATTERNS, THE BETTER YOU WILL BE AT THE GAME.

FACT FILE: LittleBIG Planet 3

If you have a PlayStation at home, or even if you've played on one at a friend's house, chances are you've come across the game LittleBigPlanet. Even if you haven't, you probably still know about their **mascot**, Sackboy, and his fabulous fabric friends.

The LittleBigPlanet games are creative platformers filled with puzzles for players to overcome using Sackboy and his amazing abilities. The main **campaign** sees you play as Sackboy, and you can collect and customize his fabric skin, clothing, hats, shoes, and even fun costumes! Running and jumping make up most of his moves, but you also have a secret weapon—the Popit menu. This menu contains everything Sackboy needs to get around his world, including new gadgets you find on your travels, and fun stickers to decorate your own little world.

Over the years, the LittleBigPlanet universe has spilled over into kart racing. There's also a game called PlayStation All-Stars Battle Royale that puts famous characters in the ring together. Sackboy's most recent appearance was in LittleBigPlanet 3, which included **co-op** play for up to four friends.

Sackboy might be best known as a platform hero, but what also makes the LittleBigPlanet series special is the freedom it gives the player. You can use a really powerful set of tools to create your own levels and games for Sackboy and his friends! In the more recent entries in the series, the tools have become really clever, including **portals** and trampolines.

CONSOLE PROFILE

While most consoles can play all types of games, there is one company whose consoles have been linked to platform games since the very beginning—Nintendo. Let's take a look at the machines behind Mario and find out more…

1977: COLOR TV-GAME 6

Small console with up to six games. Only released in Japan. 5 versions. 1–2 players.

1980: GAME & WATCH

Handheld console. One game installed. Features: clock and alarm.

1983: NINTENDO ENTERTAINMENT SYSTEM (NES)

8-**bit** TV console. First worldwide release. Sold: 61.9 million units. Games on large cartridges. Known as Famicom in Japan. Launched hugely popular games such as Donkey Kong and The Legend of Zelda.

Nintendo®

2017: NINTENDO SWITCH

Both a home console, when docked to a TV, and a portable console which functions like a tablet. Controllers known as joy-cons use movement and buttons for handheld play. Game: The Legend of Zelda: Breath of the Wild.

2012: NINTENDO WII U

A small console and tablet-like GamePad device meant that users could play either on the TV or on the handheld device's screen, or even both at once!

2006: NINTENDO WII

Wii Remotes control games through movement and buttons. Other add-ons included a steering wheel, nunchucks, tennis rackets, and guns.

1989: GAME BOY

First handheld console with cartridges and many games. Over 100 million sold. Later versions included Game Boy Light and Game Boy Color, with color graphics.

1991: SUPER NINTENDO ENTERTAINMENT SYSTEM

16-bit TV console. Best-selling console of the 16-bit **era** of video games. Sold: 49.1 million units. Upgraded some popular games and released new ones, including Super Mario Bros.

1996: NINTENDO 64 (N64)

64-bit TV console. Games: GoldenEye 007, The Legend of Zelda: Ocarina of Time.

2001: NINTENDO GAMECUBE

Games on disks, including Super Mario Sunshine, Metroid Prime, Animal Crossing, and Pikmin.

2004: NINTENDO DS

Handheld console with two screens and a **stylus**. Sold: 154 million units.

FACT FILE: STARBOUND

You've fled your home, only to discover that you're lost in space! Your only hope is to beam yourself down from your damaged ship, and hope the world below can provide everything you need to get back to sailing through the universe…

While not, strictly speaking, a platform game, exploration-based game Starbound is an action-adventure game that shares a lot with the platform genre—and breaks a lot of the rules too. Starbound is a world that players can explore freely. Unlike many platform games, players can create their own story. Will you choose to save the universe or become its ruler, **colonizing** planets and mining their resources? Maybe you'll spend your time farming the land, or rake in the virtual cash as an intergalactic landlord, renting out space to the highest bidder. The choice is yours.

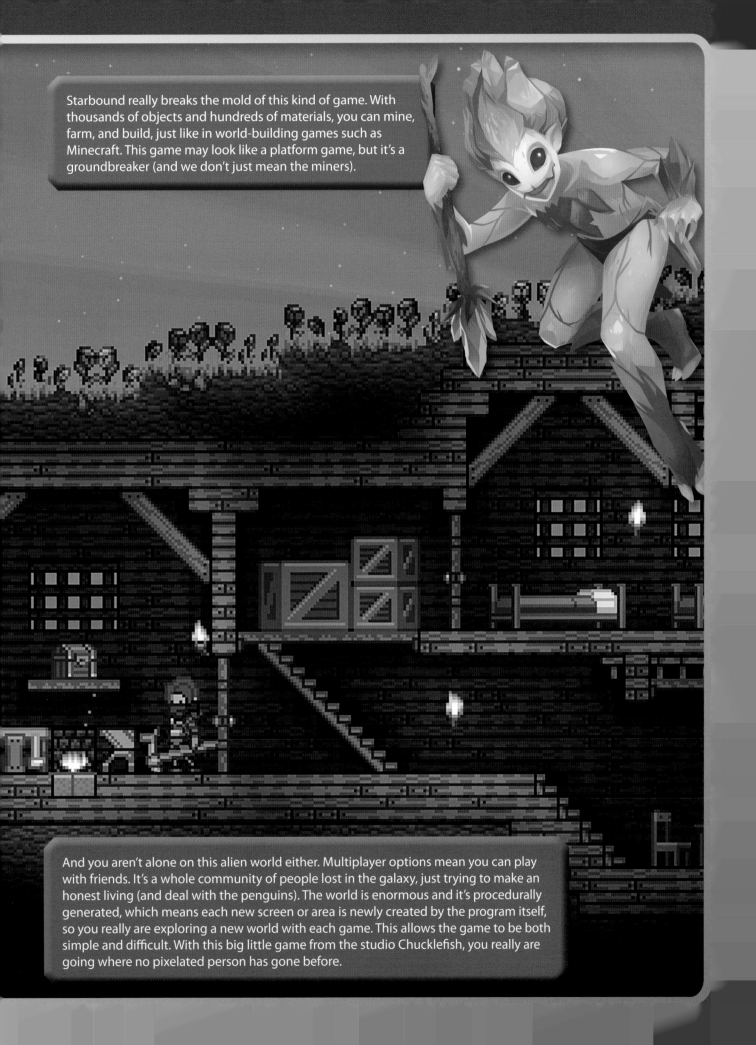

Starbound really breaks the mold of this kind of game. With thousands of objects and hundreds of materials, you can mine, farm, and build, just like in world-building games such as Minecraft. This game may look like a platform game, but it's a groundbreaker (and we don't just mean the miners).

And you aren't alone on this alien world either. Multiplayer options mean you can play with friends. It's a whole community of people lost in the galaxy, just trying to make an honest living (and deal with the penguins). The world is enormous and it's procedurally generated, which means each new screen or area is newly created by the program itself, so you really are exploring a new world with each game. This allows the game to be both simple and difficult. With this big little game from the studio Chucklefish, you really are going where no pixelated person has gone before.

PRO TALK

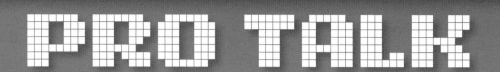

Let's find out more about games by talking to a professional. Gaming professionals do something in gaming to earn a living, such as making video games or writing about them in magazines. These pros really know their stuff. Let's hear some advice and tips from one now.

DANT RAMBO

Writer and producer at Choice Provisions. When he's not working on the **narrative** for a game, he's making sure everyone on the team gets their work done on time. It's a pretty good life.

1. WHAT MAKES GAMES FUN TO PLAY WITH YOUR FRIENDS?

"We really tend to lean towards multiplayer games that make us laugh. Games like Overcooked, WarioWare, and Mario Kart come to mind, because they're all games you can have fun with whether you win or lose. The fun is baked right into the formula, making them surefire bets when looking for a game to play with your friends."

2. WHY DO WE LIKE CHALLENGING AND DIFFICULT GAMES?

"Accomplishing something challenging is always a great feeling, and with games in particular, it's easy to see yourself improve as you play. Struggling with a boss? Chances are you'll do a little bit better each time you fight it. You continue to improve as you continue to play, until finally you manage to pull it off."

3. WHAT MAKES A GREAT VIDEO GAME CHARACTER?

"A character that helps the player connect to the game they're playing. Even if the character is silly, evil, or completely silent, you want the player to connect with them in some way. Of course, it always helps if the player sees a little of themselves in the character they're playing as. This is why **representation** in games is so important."

4. WHAT CAN GAMES DO THAT OTHER MEDIUMS CAN'T?

"The interactive nature of games allows them to affect people in ways other **mediums** aren't able to. A video game has the opportunity to not only ask the player a question, but allow them the chance to answer it. Video games let you be a part of the story, and to see an outcome based on your own actions can make for a great lesson in **empathy**."

5. HOW CAN GAMES HELP US BE MORE CREATIVE?

"I personally think most games have the ability to encourage creativity. This is especially true in modern games, which more often than not provide the player with several different options as to how they want to make their way through the game. This encourages creative decision-making, which is a skill that is very important in the real world!"

6. HOW DO YOU BALANCE SIMULATION WITH FUN?

"That's a tricky question! For us, our focus with every game we release is on making it as fun as possible. Most of us on the team like silly, unrealistic games, which in turn inspires us to make silly games of our own. Everyone's idea of fun is different, so it comes down to a matter of taste. For us, however, we strive to make the funnest, goofiest games we possibly can."

WORK AND PLAY

Do you like playing video games? When you grow up, wouldn't that be a cool job? Did you know that you can actually work on video games? Yes, that's right, people will pay you to play games! But that's not all. There are lots of jobs in gaming, and it's more than just playing games. Let's find out more...

THE JOB SHOP

EXTRA! EXTRA!

The video game industry is so large that it has its own journalists. Journalists are people who know a LOT about video games and write about them in newspapers and magazines and on websites. They get to meet people who work in gaming, interview them, and write about them afterward. If you like games and writing, then this could be the job for you!

GOOD INFLUENCE

Some people, called influencers, play and talk about video games online, on streaming sites such as YouTube and Twitch. They get paid for this through **sponsors** and advertising.

GET WITH THE PROGRAM

Programmers write the code that makes the game work. They use different computer languages to tell the game what to do. If you like math, computers, and coding, you'll love getting paid to do this!

ONCE UPON A TIME

Narrative designers write stories, characters, and levels for games. Big games such as Skyrim or Mass Effect have lots of narrative designers working together, while smaller games might only have one! If you like stories, this could be a great job for you.

WORK OF ART

Graphic designers create the visuals for a game. They draw the scenery, characters, and maps for games and give them a distinctive style. If you like drawing, painting, and art, as well as games, you'd love this job.

PAID TO PLAY

Once a game is made, someone has to check that it's all working properly. Playtesters play games in the early stages to look for difficulty, problems, and story issues. If you like playing games and you're very, very thorough, you'll enjoy this job.

IN PUBLIC

People in public relations (PR) tell the public and journalists about the games they represent. They create interesting ads, talk to the press, and tell everyone how brilliant their games are. If you're friendly, chatty, and social, and a bit creative, you'll love working in PR.

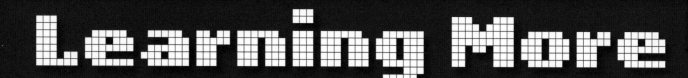

Learning More

You made it to the end! Well done. We can leave the Arcade now if you want to, and go play some amazing platform games. Or, if you're not finished learning, you can go to these websites to find out more...

<<CONTINUE? Y/N>>
HTTP://PLAYSTARBOUND.COM/

<<CONTINUE? Y/N>>
WWW.SEGA.COM

<<CONTINUE? Y/N>>
WWW.PLAYSTATION.COM/EN-US/
GAMES/LITTLEBIGPLANET-3-PS4/

<<CONTINUE? Y/N>>
WWW.RUNNER3.GAME/

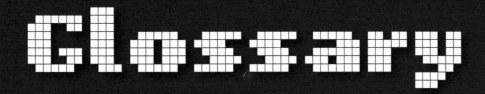

Glossary

3-D	Short for three-dimensional, an object that has height, length, and width
battle royale	A fight with many players that ends when only one player remains
bit	The smallest unit of information in a computer
campaign	A continuing storyline or set of adventures
colonize	When a place or nation controls another area and its people
console	A computer system that connects video games to a screen
co-op	Short for cooperative, a video game that lets players play as teammates
defined	To give the accepted meaning to something
electronic	Describes a device or machine powered by electricity
empathy	Identifying with or sharing the feelings of someone else
era	A set period of time
generation	Groups of things or people that are roughly the same age
genre	A particular type of something
graphics	Images and design on a computer screen
invincible	Cannot be defeated
mascot	A person, animal, or character that symbolizes an event or organization
medium	A particular form or system of communication
narrative	The storyline or sequence of actions in a game
nimble	Quick and light in movement and action
objective	The main goal or target
obstacles	Things that get in the way and must be overcome
pixelated	An electronic image made up of small squares which can be seen
portal	A window or doorway to another level or world
power-up	A bonus a player can collect to give their character an advantage
reflexes	The natural ability to react quickly
representation	When people of different races are visibly present in the media
sponsor	A person or organization who supplies money for a project
strategy	A plan, or series of actions, that will achieve a desired outcome
stylus	A writing instrument for use with screens or video games
tutorial	A teaching level in which gamers learn the controls for a particular game
virtual	Something that seems to exist but was created by a computer

Index